The Lady's E(Manual)
By Carla Tilghman
Cover Created by Jazzy Kitty Publications
Front Cover Designed by Carla Tilghman/Kaitlin Johnson
Logo Designs by Andre M. Saunders/Jess Zimmerman
Editor: Anelda L. Attaway

© 2020 Carla Tilghman
ISBN 978-1-7357874-1-1
Library of Congress Control Number: 2020918266

All rights reserved. This book is protected by the copyright laws of the United States of America. This book may not be copied or reprinted for commercial gain or profit. The use of short quotations or occasional page copying for personal or group study is permitted and encouraged. Permission will be granted upon request. This book is for Worldwide Distribution and printed in the United States of America, published by Jazzy Kitty Publications utilizing Microsoft Publishing Software.

DEDICATIONS

I would like to dedicate this book to all the beautiful Queens in my life who sacrificed for me, instilled wisdom within me, and who picked me up time and time again.

Mommy, aka Elder, aka Mim, thank you for all your sacrifices for me. Now that I have a better understanding of myself and the world around me, I understand that being a mother isn't the easiest thing in the world. It requires a lot of sacrifices, a lot of patience, and a whole lot of prayer. I want to thank you, Mommy, from the bottom of my heart for always doing the best you can with me, even during times when it seems as though I'm very critical of you. My eyes have been opened to what it means to be a woman of God and I can see that you are a woman of God, a distinguished lady of standard and a blessing in my life. I thank God that He gave me you as a mother, a supporter, a provider, and a best friend.

Lisa Johnson, when I met you at age 15-years-old, I didn't know that just being in your presence and under your teaching would ultimately affect the entire course of my life. Your spirit, your seeds of wisdom, and your aurora have watered the seeds within me even to have the confidence to flourish and blossom, let alone write a book. I am so grateful for the conversations that we have where you take the time to really listen to my heart. I remember sharing my journals and thoughts with you, and you gave me the idea to write this book. I didn't think I had it in me, but after having conversations with you, I was inspired by your confidence in me to take a leap of faith and just as you taught me before God met me where I was and took the wheel.

Thank you for always believing in me and honoring the light that lives within you.

ACKNOWLEDGMENTS

I would like first to thank God and honor His divine presence, which has changed the outcome of my life. God, I thank you for loving me through all of my seasons and for helping me to release my past so I could embrace the future you have envisioned for me. Thank you for never giving up on me, even when I had given up on myself.

I would like to thank my friends, Mariel and Delma, who I would constantly send rough drafts of my book and always asking their opinion and ideas. Mariel, thank you for weathering some of the storms with me and for being a friend who I could always depend on for good counsel.

I would like to thank both of my grandmothers for being pillars of strength and laughter for me. Mom-mom, aka Ro-boogie with the hoodie LOL I love you and thank you for taking care of me in ways I didn't even know about until I became an adult. You have a special place in my heart. My Gimes, thank you for not being a typical grandmother and keeping me on my toes! Your love has gotten me through some of my darkest moments. Thank you both for your life.

I would like to thank my sisters: Danielle, Brittani, and Alexis, for continuously supporting me. Alexis, I love your "Gang Gang*/" spirit, and I need more of that in my life. Thank you for showing me love and being a shoulder to cry on even when you're not in the mood. Brittani, you are a hard worker and dedicated to living your life to the fullest as you travel the world. Speaking of that, don't forget to invite me!! Danielle, you are the light of my life. Thank you for praying with me and telling me I'm beautiful and that the 'real me' is awesome.

Lastly, I would like to thank my family, friends, and all those who supported me through this life-changing experience. All your work did not go unnoticed and without you, I couldn't have written this. LOVE Y'ALL LOTS.

TABLE OF CONTENTS

PROLOGUE	i
STEP 1 - Get Up 10	01
STEP 2 – Trust My Lonely Uncertainty	05
STEP 3 – I Need to Change My Diet.	11
STEP 4 – My Journey to the Big C (Celibacy)	15
STEP 5 – Learn to Listen	22
STEP 6 – Break the Cycles	29
STEP 7 – A Devine Connection	35
EPILOGUE	40
ABOUT THE AUTHOR	41

PROLOGUE

"I'm declaring war between you and the woman, between your offspring and hers. He'll wound your head; you'll wound his heel."

Being a woman is not easy. We're naturally more emotionally intuitive; we care hard and love harder. When it's time to close chapters of our lives in relationships, friendships, or those tricky situationships, we tend to experience the after-effects in a more personal way. Sometimes our self-image gets distorted because you're trying to make sense why someone doesn't want you the way you want them. Our self-esteem may take a turn for the worst because deep down, we're searching to be loved. I understand because as I'm writing to you, I'm experiencing everything I just mentioned.

I used to believe that because I believed in Jesus, prayed, and recited my affirmations that I would be immune to another broken heart. Yet, life hit me, and I had to readjust and pick myself up again. At that moment, I realized that for me to move forward in my life, I needed to understand that the weapons against me will form. As we grow and enter new dimensions of our lives, pain will be a part of the process, no matter how sanctified, holy, or deep you are.

God never said, "Because you follow Me, you will be immune from pain." So, where did I get this idea? I'm still trying to figure that out!

But God-sister, I say this to say although we can't stop the weapons from forming, the man from leaving, the best friend from walking away, and the bills from piling up, these things will never prosper. Your strength comes from your soul. It does not come from makeup, or how many men want you, or how slim-thick your waist is. As a woman, our strength is tested in many different ways, which is why our war is just a little bit different than men. The enemy has a personal war with you because there's nothing more powerful than a woman who owns herself and knows you may wound her heel, but she can still crush your head. Sometimes you have to pick up and leave situations scarred, broken, and bruised, but even on your worst day, you have the power to defeat any weapon that may form in your life.

So as we begin and embark on this journey, I want to remind you to be KIND and gentle with yourself. Change is hard. We're going to be breaking down old mindsets, re-creating new perspectives, and discover different ways to renew our minds so we can be the best version of ourselves. It's not easy, but with time every day presents a new opportunity to grow. At first, it may feel like you're breaking, but I'd like you to think of this as *breaking free.* You are intentionally freeing yourself from old patterns of thinking, behaviors, and insecurities voicing their opinions for far too long. So a little PSA to those old ways: Your days are numbered...

This guide is for the broken-hearted woman who is searching for her healing. It's for the woman who's always been told she was beautiful, but never really felt she was beautiful. This guide is for the woman who knows her worth and understands no one can validate her worth. This guide is for the woman who dreams of one day having everything she prayed for and has faith that God can do it, but sometimes what she sees with her physical eyes makes her doubt what God can do. Hang in there, God-sis, this guide is for you and me...

Thing to Remember

- *It's not about the day; it's about the pattern*
- *Change is hard*
- *Every day you are growing*
- *Even on your worst days, you are worth it*
- *You are not who left you*
- *You have the power to decide what you will take to the next dimension of your life*
- *Your obedience grows your heart*
- *The bet is still on!*
- *Your language creates your reality. (change your language)*
- *Yes, you can*
- *If at first, you don't succeed...dust yourself off and try again. - Aaliyah*
- *Nothing is only bad or good*
- *Anything that you are not willing to change becomes a habit*
- *You can trust God and go to therapy...*
- *There's power in what you pay attention to*

STEP 1

Get Up 10

In the words from one of my favorite artists Cardi B: "Look myself in the mirror, I say we gon' win knock me down 9 times but I get up 10!" If you haven't listened to the song I highly recommend it. There are so many good life messages in the song. One of the first things I would like to talk to you about is having a Get Up 10 mindset. What is that? A Get Up 10 mindset is an attitude or belief that there is nothing this world can throw at you that you can't recover from. Absolutely frickin nothing. It's an inner power that's silent but very much present. Your man left, you can recover. Your job let you go, you can recover. Your friends switched up, you can recover. Your finances are tight, you can recover. Your living situation is unstable, you can recover. You just got the most unexpected news of your life and you have no idea what to do, where to go, how this is going to work out...IT IS OKAY because YOU CAN RECOVER. As a child of God, as His princess, as His daughter we have been given a special power: a connection to God.

Personally, I see God as a never-ending waterfall of resources and minerals that I can drink from, shower in and tap into any time. So when life tries to tire me out and beat me down I retreat to my personal waterfall and sip from His everlasting water. It encourages me even with tears streaming down my face to get back up again. As I mentioned earlier friends, just because we are children of God does not exclude us from getting thrown off and knocked down while we're going through this thing called LIFE. However, as a child of God we have access to a "forever strength", enduring sustainability, eternal peace, eternal healing, unlimited freedom, agape LOVE, joy, and laughter even during the bad times. For instance, a short time ago, I was disappointed by a man again. Yes again. I was so confused because I was more intentional than I had EVER been. I wasn't clingy, overthinking, and I was finally communicating in a healthier way than I had in my past. When he left me I felt rejected all over again and I felt my heart was defeated. Here I am trying to grow and be a woman of God but these men in my life keep walking away from me. What is wrong with me? I remember I cried in my bed while I was on the phone with my god sister Mariel. I was crying for at least 2 hours now and I had class in the next 15 minutes. In my pain I said I wasn't going to class because at the moment I couldn't think clearly. The moment I mentioned I couldn't go to class this wave of Cardi's song came over me and then I began to whisper "Knock me down 9 times but I'll get up 10." This was definitely a hurt piece and knocked me flat on my back but something (maybe Cardi, Mariel or even Jesus) said "No my love, get up 10." Now, I would be a liar if I said I put on some makeup and went to class and that was that. NOT EVEN CLOSE. I cried as I put on my makeup, I cried as I went to class and in class I shed a few tears and had to excuse myself to just take a breath. I am so proud that I kept going though. This shows it doesn't matter how you get back up, just get up.

God-sis life can knock you down sometimes and it may take longer to get up, and that's okay. Everyone's journey is different, you and I may not share the same pain but what we do share is one God, one source, one piece of eternal energy that will shine through if you surrender to it and choose to activate it. And God-sis, even though I got up in that moment and still went to class I cried every day for at least 3 weeks after that.

However, every day I made the decision to welcome whatever pain would come and I was determined to move through it in order to overcome it. It takes courage, heart, discipline and vulnerability to move through pain. You must allow yourself to feel it and not gloss over it because God will intentionally allow something to happen to teach you something about yourself. Pay attention, wake up, and fight that battle and believe you have it within you to overcome anything this life will try to throw at you. So get up swinging, get up with tears, get up with snot coming out your nose, get up depressed, get up unsure, get up afraid, get up angry, get up hopeless, get up confused, get up heartbroken....JUST get up. Make the mental decision today, in this moment, as you are reading this sentence that there is nothing in life that you cannot recover from and like Cardi you'll get up 10.

Phrase: Write a phrase from this chapter that stood out to you. How is it going to help you?

STEP 2

Trust My Lonely Uncertainty

Through some of life's teachings, a few disappointments, and a surprising heartbreak, I made a vow to myself that I would rather be alone than connected to the wrong spirit. All I wanted to do was stop the pain that I was experiencing, which resulted from allowing people to get close enough to hurt me. As a "younger" lady, I swore I would never allow my heart to be so hardened to the point where I would not allow real love to enter my life. The idea of having love and rejecting it scared me more than finding "love" and dealing with the emotions of it slipping away. So what did I do? I kept my heart open and available to everything. I had faith that I was not going to make the common mistake by allowing people to pay for mistakes they did not make. While my intention may have been right, the way I went about it was WRONG: I ignored red flags, ignored my better judgment, and overlooked many things that I knew weren't right. And in the end, I was left adapting physically, emotionally, and mentally to another person's absence. So after a while, I vowed I would rather be alone than be attached to the wrong people. Initially, this sentiment brought me peace. I was elated not being bothered, knowing without a doubt that I'm not being cheated on. I was not worrying about if I'm good enough and focusing on me. And sis, I'm talking about really being alone (no sex, no "potentials" (guys that you're thinking about dating), no men other than my dad texting my phone. I worked two jobs, was a full-time graduate student, and during my free time, I either studied or watched movies in my little dorm room. Being alone helped me connect to ME. I got to understand at a deeper level who Carla is all while learning my strength. Trust me; there are some things I never thought I would bounce back from that I did. But after about three months or so of self-reflecting, healing, and journaling, I found myself sad. At first, I didn't know what it was, but as I explored the feeling and processed my inner thoughts, I came to a surprising conclusion: I felt LONELY. Correction: I feel lonely. Yes, I decided to change my narrative and not settle for anything less than I deserve, but I didn't feel better. And this didn't just apply to relationships; it applied to my friendships. I no longer wanted to be in one-sided situations where I felt I was the only one giving. I let the old, toxic things go and manifested new relationships, friendships, partnerships, jobs, and business relationships.

Although I felt that I was growing, I wasn't ready to face the possibility of what waiting meant. In three months, loneliness came over me like a shadow, and I started feeling sorry for myself, wishing I had stayed where I was. I would think, "Yeah, it was bad, but at least I wasn't lonely." It reminds me of one famous story in the Bible when Moses set the Israelites free from Egypt. After the Israelites left slavery and started going to the Promised Land, the road to their destiny got a little bumpy along the way. Like really bumpy, running into the Red Sea, getting distracted, staying in the same spot for 40 years, and a lot of uncertainty about where their next meal was coming from. During their tribulation, they decided they would have rather stayed in Egypt. Imagine that. They would have preferred to stay in bondage where they were beaten, abused, taken advantage of, diminished, broken, hopeless, and begging to be free than to keep moving through the uncertainty to God's promise. I want you to know, I understand. I'm not here to judge or criticize you. I'm not saying I've been there and moved past that. I'm telling you I'm here in this moment, and every day is a challenge to get up and move forward. Unsure of whether or not I'll be in love again, I'll learn to trust again and if I'll open my heart again to be vulnerable. In moments like this, sometimes going back to what you know, to the comfort, to the *certainty* seems more appealing than what it actually is.

Although there are many aspects of my life that I am uncertain of, there is one certainty that keeps me grounded: the present pain I feel now cannot compare to the joy that's to come. Even though I can't see it, I have faith that God will not leave me here. He has not forgotten me. I know my best days are not behind me, and to reach a new dimension, I have to go through the process of feeling lonely, uncertain, and at times disappointed.

The story of the Israelites getting out of Egypt illustrates to me that sometimes it can be easier for God to remove us from our Egypt (our place of bondage) than for us to let our Egypt go mentally. I've also come to learn that life is about balance and perspective. How can I appreciate the highs if I never experience the lows? It is also in my lowest of lows that I feel the most profound connection to God. It's as if my heart is so open that I'm sensitive to His lightest touch. He touches me in such a way that I'm compelled to keep moving forward, inspired to keep reaching for things I can't see, and motivated to push beyond my present emotions. I may be uncertain about a lot of things, but God is not one of them. As I heard my Bishop say in his sermon, "I serve a God who specializes in brokenness." It is in my brokenness where I'm fluid enough for Him to mold me, shape me, and build me into a woman I never thought I could be, but who God always knew I was. So I couldn't return to my old habits and old relationships because I was reminded of why I left in the first place. The instant gratification wouldn't bring me the unconditional love that was I yearning. I had already tested that theory multiple times before. I knew deep in my heart that I could not do the same thing and expect different results. And I knew the things I wanted like love, healing, freedom, forgiveness, and confidence was something I shouldn't have searched for in people but what I needed to learn to give myself. So I asked God to give me the strength to surrender so He could teach me how to love myself so I can love others. I asked Him to remove the pain, disappointments, and bitterness from my heart and replace it with healing, forgiveness, joy, and understanding. It was only in my brokenness and uncertainty that I could open my heart fully without restraint to my Maker. And God-sis, He met me right where I was. I mean, MET ME. He didn't criticize me, chastise me, or hold it against me. He supported me, He held me, He comforted me, and He loves me through it all. Every day He meets me in my uncertainty and shows me that He is my beautiful certainty.

You may not be ready to dive into a lonely uncertainty, and that's okay. I will never judge you for wanting to be loved and feel safe. I understand. That's why it took me almost six months to get away from one man. I thought I loved how he made me feel, but truthfully, I was too afraid to see what my world would look like without him in it. I wasn't ready to move forward. I didn't trust God, and I didn't trust myself. But one day, after going through the same thing over and over and over again, I became more afraid of the woman I was allowing myself to become. The fear of staying the same outweighed the fear of change. I knew there had to be better. God-sis, I don't know what your lonely may look like to you because it looks different for everyone. But let me assure you...you can make it. You are braver, stronger, and more powerful than you know. I believe in you, and more importantly, God believes in you. So take a chance, trust your lonely, and know that He is all the certainty you need.

In the words of Alessia Cara, "My world is brighter by itself and I can do better...do better ALONE."

Reflection: Think about a time when you were alone. How did it feel? What scared you? What helped you? Do you believe God is your beautiful certainty? Why or why not?

STEP 3

I Need to Change My Diet

The other day, I was listening to an interview on Ciara Wilson. She talked about everything that led her to make her extraordinary album *Beauty Marks,* the journey she endured as a single woman, and how she manifested her husband, Russel Wilson. Yes, it *manifested* her husband as she believed and meditated so heavily on what she wanted that it showed up in her life. The power of manifestation is real God-sis. Anyway, during her interview, something she said caught my attention more than anything.

She said, "I prayed for what I needed."

For some reason, this caught my attention. At first, I thought, *"Well, of course, you prayed for what you needed, what else would you pray for?"* Then I thought about the words she used. She intentionally used "needed" not "wanted."

As I reflected further, it dawned on me that I never once prayed for what I *needed* in a partner but always for what I wanted. I definitely knew what I wanted: a good looking man, nice eyes, good sense of humor, respect, good in the bedroom, etc. But what did I need? What would feed my soul, what would draw me to a man spiritually? What would create a sustainable relationship? And since we're transparent God-sis, to be honest, I did not know. I didn't have an answer. And through me not knowing, a question burned through my mind day in and day out: How can I get the man I want if I don't know what I need?

In my season of being alone, I was able to get honest with myself and process what I need from a man. The desire to taste something different inspired me to figure out what it is I needed. So God needed to change my diet. I needed Him to change my taste for things. I could no longer crave a man out of loneliness or lust for the empty instant gratifications. I didn't want to thirst for kind, flattering words with empty actions behind them. I didn't want just sweet, sugary, dynamic one night relations because, after a while, it made me sick. And guess what happened? While searching, I discovered that if I get what I need, I'll get what I *want*. That's what Ciara was talking about! If she got what she needed in a man, she would get what she wanted.

This process also made it very easy to weed out what was for me and what was not. In my mind, if you're not giving me what I need, you definitely don't have what I want. And since God is a God of overflow and abundance, not only did God reveal what I needed, but he showed me *why* I needed it. I learned at that moment I can't just say what I need; I have to understand why I need it. For example, the very first thing I realized I needed was a man that has a relationship with God. While this has been something that has been said all my life, it was the first time it made sense. I am rooted in God; therefore, a man who is not rooted in God would ultimately uproot me. And for the first time, God showed me the men I gave myself to in the past did not have a relationship with Him. They knew of Him, but there's a difference between knowing someone and having a relationship with them. Through this revelation, I was able to heal because I was certain there was no way it could've worked with these men, and it's a blessing they let me go. Mentally, these men and I were not on the same page, so the only thing connecting me to them was physical gratification. And God-sis, that wasn't a connection but codependency. We'll get to that a little later...

As Lauryn Hill so beautifully sings: *"Thought what I wanted was something I needed."* I say this to show you sometimes what you want is not always what you need. Instead of solely focusing on what you want, focus on what you need. Focus on what will sustain you, focus on what gives you a spark, and what will make the spark last. Trust me, sex can only go for so long, and after a while, it's just pointless because you're no longer getting anything but a few moments of pleasure for a long headache later. Look inside yourself, ask God what it is that you need, listen, seek Him, and watch Him give you what you want.

Reflection: What is it that you need in a significant other? Have you ever prayed for what you need?

STEP 4

My Journey to the Big C (Celibacy)

Before you close your mind, heart, and this book (because that's exactly what I did whenever anyone mentioned celibacy to me), I want you to hear me out for a moment, okay? I am not perfect, nor am I super-duper Holy, sanctified, and I surely am not one to preach to you.

However, I am a beautiful, open-minded 25 year *young* (not old) woman who has gotten beauty marks from her experiences and would love to share with others what God has done for me and hopefully help you navigate through your life not to make the same mistakes. I did not get here overnight, and I fell a bunch of times along the way, which has brought me to this point: not a perfect point, not an "I'm better than you" point, but a level of wisdom and understanding that although I may fall I will try my best not to.

However, before we continue, I would like to acknowledge that sex may look different to you than it does for me. Maybe you were abused, taken advantage of, hurt, forced, coerced, or influenced into performing an act you didn't want to do. If this is you God-sis, from the bottom of my heart, I am sorry. I do not share your pain and will not, for one second, pretend that I do. I believe you have a strength that is unparalleled to anyone on this earth. You have carried this weight and whatever has been attached to that weight. What I do know is that there is a God that dwells within you that can love you past your pain and who can provide eternal healing. Seek Him. And if you need help mentally, please see if therapy is something you can do. You are in charge of your healing, your happiness, and your life. Do not allow anyone else's opinions to rob you of getting what you need to live your best life.

My journey with celibacy began less than a year ago, so once again, I'm not the expert, but I know what works for me. I tried celibacy because I needed to cleanse my mind, body, and spirit. Regardless of what people may say or believe that "sex is just sex," there is a bond that you create with a person once you give yourself to them. And at this point in my life, I had created bonds with people that I had no business dealing with in the first place. I used sex to connect. I felt that a man would choose me if I gave myself to him. Unfortunately, sex became the sole foundation of many situationships, and eventually, the only thing keeping that person and me together was the physical gratification.

I was searching to be loved, to be chosen, and at the time, it really helped calm me down but only for a moment. It became a dangerous attachment when the man still wouldn't choose me, but I would continue to give myself to him in the hopes of him changing his mind and to fill a void. In my mind, sex made the relationship. So if I wanted this to work, I had to keep giving. The problem for me was the feelings and emotions that are attached to sex. I was emotionally tied to this person. I kept giving up my power, and eventually, that person would have control over me. It was causing me to be in one-sided relationships and situationships, time and time again. Mentally, this made me feel like I wasn't good enough. Emotionally, I was all over the place because I was so tied up with a man who didn't want me but wanted sex. Physically, it made me crave sex so much the thought of leaving terrified me because I wanted to keep the feeling. And spiritually, it took me further and further away from God. It was a poisonous time in my life; I kept sleeping with the thing that was killing me. I kept entertaining B.S. because the thought of being alone was the absolute worst thing in my mind. I was exhausted mentally, up and down emotionally, physically, never satisfied, and spiritually empty. At times, I couldn't even bring myself to talk to God because I knew what I was doing, and it made me feel worthless.

As I reflect on what I went through, I can see I was spiraling. I was diving deeper and deeper into hopelessness. Instead of facing my disappointment, insecurities, and broken heart head-on, I learned to live and operate around my pain. As Sarah Jakes Roberts so beautifully mentions in her message, I was mentally in a place where I couldn't take another loss, so I held on to the dysfunction I had. I couldn't afford to lose anymore. But God showed me time and time again that what I was giving was too costly. I knew what needed to be done, but I wasn't ready nor willing to do it. So God allowed me to become desperate, and it was in my desperation that my soul cried out to God. I was never satisfied, and I got tired of dealing with the headaches. I got tired of not feeling good enough. I got tired of losing. And most of all, I got tired of becoming empty.

Yet, as I look back, I see my emptiness saved my life and continues to save me today. Even in my emptiness, in that hollow place, that void within me, there was a voice that was urging me, beckoning me, calling me to walk away. This soft, still, calming voice kept telling me that I had to let it all go because eventually, if I kept going down this road of destruction, I would end up pregnant or catching an STD. I could taste the woman I wanted to be if I could just break this stronghold off of me.

So I had to choose: Do I continue down this road of temporary fulfillments, or do I lay this down to be better?

And the enemy kept bothering me, saying, "How do you know it will get better? How do you know God can heal you? How do you know He's even there? You might as well stay where you are. You can't do it."

In the midst, I kept hearing God say, "I got you, I won't let you down. I can help you, but you have to let Me. I have more for you. You can do this; just trust Me."

I wish I could tell you that I chose God, and it was smooth sailing from then on out. But it wasn't. At first, I felt grief for the people I knew I would have to disconnect from my life. I would have to disconnect from certain friends, not because there was something wrong with them, but because I couldn't handle the temptation. I mourned because I knew if I didn't give this person sex, then he would ultimately walk away from me. Though I can look back now and see that person was never for me and am grateful it happened, at the moment, you may not feel the joy or understand that it's a blessing. In the moment, it feels like another loss. But God reminded me of something. Since I was a child, I had learned that all things work together for the good for those who love Him and are called according to His purpose. So I knew this pain I was feeling on this side of the blood was working for me. I was desperate and thirsty for change, and when my desperation met an intentional God, He was able to show me that He gave me a "by any means necessary" mindset. This mindset made me believe it didn't matter what pain I would come; I just knew it could not be greater than the pain I was already accepting. I had finally realized that for too long, I was accustomed to living around my disappointment, and the only way to get beyond where I was to become the woman heaven had in mind, to attract the man God had intended for me I desperately needed to change. I could no longer get caught up emotionally with these men, but I needed to get caught up emotionally with God. I had opened up myself to these men and never opened myself up to God.

I got tired of adjusting to people's absence and instead decided to have faith in the man who said He would never leave me. My journey became easier. At first, I dealt with the cravings of wanting sex, and sometimes I would stay up a night because the urge was so strong. Eventually, I left and moved to Atlanta, Georgia, to pursue my master's degree. I chose a different city because I wanted to start fresh with my walk. It was the hardest decision because it felt final to me; there was no room to be uncertain because all my temptations were home. I was scared, uncertain, and jumped without wings, but it was one of the best decisions I ever made because I earned my wings on the way down.

In my celibacy, I have gotten a taste of who God is for myself, not for who my grandmother knows Him to be, who my mother knows Him to be, but I know Him for myself, and I thank God every day that He waited for me. I can disconnect emotionally and mentally from certain things and see the bigger picture. Now I can look back and see why certain things weren't working for me. It has also allowed me to clean up my emotions. Reading books like "The Wait" by Devon Franklin and Meagan Good and "The Single Woman" by Mandy Hale was perfect for me during the time because it kept reminding me of my *why*. Why am I choosing to be celibate? Because I want God's best for me. I don't want to settle and have emotional ties with people I don't need to have those ties. "The Wait" taught me that when you are with someone that God did not intend for you, some sort of pain is inevitable. And this had reigned true in my life. I stopped feeding into the culture and what everyone else was doing and did what worked for me. I would watch Sarah Jakes Roberts sermons, read, explore my new city, I saw a spiritual counselor, I watched new shows, I climbed mountains, I tried new foods, I learned different recipes, and I dedicated myself to my new profession, which is all about healing people. I walked away from one thing and was given so much more.

God-sis, you have GOT to be willing to lay something down. If you know it's not prospering you, lay it down before God. Ask God to put His touch on it. God can turn that pain into purpose, pain into passion, the heartbreak into healing, weariness into replenishment, and emptiness into overflow. Don't get caught up for years in toxic, dysfunctional situationships. Stop entertaining the thing that is killing you. At the moment, your world might be surrounded by that one thing, that one person, that one moment, and the thought of losing it just seems too great. But there is nothing too big for God. No stronghold can overtake Him. Walk in the certainty that God will meet you right where you are during your pain and give you way more than you can imagine.

Question: What are you willing to lay down to become the best version of you?

STEP 5

Learn to Listen

As I was beginning to get back to my core, my center, the woman God called me to be, I began to hear His voice more clearly. My spirit was able to sense His, and from this developed a beautiful, clear communication. I was beginning to feel God and feel what was right for me and what wasn't. As I strengthened my relationship with God, I had faith that since I was putting Him first and honoring Him with my body, mind, and soul that the man He destined for me was not too far away. I was anxious in a sense, and through this next experience, I would learn why God clearly says, "Be anxious for nothing..." My desire to be in a relationship, to be a wife, lead me to believe my next relationship would be my last. In a sense, this was true; it was the last time I would allow myself to be connected to the wrong spirit. As I look back to this small but meaningful encounter, I can see this man really broke me but put me back into alignment with God, which God-sis is the best place you can be.

When I met him, I believed I was operating in a new state of mind. I dedicated myself to celibacy and trusting God every step of the way. No matter what came, rain, or shine, I devoted myself to Him. And shortly after, here comes a man claiming to be a prince. He intrigued my interest, I must say. He had a smooth demeanor, and he was persistent, but I knew I wanted to do things differently. So I kept distance between us. I made sure I didn't invest all of my time into him too early as I had done before. At first, he was charming, and he gave me attention, called often, brought me lunch to my job, and was my date to my job's Christmas Party. I thought it all made sense like I was supposed to be with him. But there was something about him that I could not overlook; it was his anger. Whenever he got mad or something annoyed him, he would snap. He would get out of character and bring all sorts of attention to himself, then apologize to me later, telling me he cared for me, and he was going to work on it. I believed him, but I also thought I could help him. Here I am studying clinical mental health, and I'm dating a man who appears to have anger issues. Maybe I could practice emotional regulation or take him to church where he could address the problem. I thought I could support him and still date him. However, something just wasn't sitting right.

See God-sis; here I am telling myself that when I meet the man God has for me when I talk about him, my face will light up, and I'll just feel all this warmth and love. Yet, that didn't happen with this man. When I brought up that I was dating, I was very unsure of whether I should continue to date him. His anger was an issue, he still wasn't over his ex, and there was one date where he left me and went to her because she was in trouble. Yeah, "trouble." In addition to this, he was up and down emotionally. I knew I couldn't take this for long and that I needed better. I just didn't know how to let go because I believed with all my heart that my next relationship would be my last. Yet, here I am, so unsure and questioning myself AGAIN because he was inconsistent. As I discussed this with a trusted college admin, she simply asked me a question that laid everything to rest.

She said so calmly but firmly, "Carla, is he good for your spirit?"

I had no response, which was my answer. The fact that I couldn't answer this question revealed that I needed to let this go. Therefore, I told him that I needed to talk with him, he said he didn't want to talk (which was more confirmation that he wasn't for me). At that point, I had carried so much anger in from being patient and trying to be understanding with you but then realizing you won't take the time of day to listen to me! I LET IT LOOSE! All sorts of curses and slurs flew out of my mouth that day. I was furious!

However, I wasn't furious with him; I was furious with myself. That unsettling feeling I had for weeks about something not being right was God telling me to let this go before it got worse. It was my spirit telling me that this person is not compatible with your mind, body, and spirit, and being with him would ultimately subtract from your life. Although I was hearing, I wasn't listening, which caused God to put a period on a sentence I didn't have the strength to end.

After the situation had ended, I still went through so much pain mentally, emotionally, and spiritually adjusting to his absence. Still, it was one of the best things that ever happened to me. He sent me on a path that realigned me with God. Even though it hurt, it made me depend on God much more than I already had because I had found that in Him, I felt safe, secure, and protected. So I longed to feel that again. I yearned for that safety with Jesus and vowed never to put myself in this kind of situation again. I told myself I would never feel *that* again, and in my determination, I forced myself to level up. I changed my perspective of being hurt to simply leveling up. One way I leveled up was accepting that this helped me more than it hurt me. See what I have come to learn is you choose what you take into the next dimensions of your life. Instead of focusing on how I was feeling and how angry I was, I fueled all that negative energy into a positive and thought of all the things it was teaching me; and God-sis this taught me a lot. First, I learned that not everything is only good or bad. However, we train our minds to see in black and white, it's either this or that, but life offers us a variety of colors and perspectives if you are willing to look. This situation was not only good or bad. It was a failure that I allowed to be another stepping stone to greatness. So while I was feeling all the negatives, I got more specific with my prayers of what I needed in a man. I wrote it down and meditated on it day in and day out. I also decided to do a spiritual cleanse. It was lent around this time, so I decided to cleanse myself of social media, procrastination. I gave up speaking negatively, complaining, as well as overthinking, and thinking about being alone. The ending of that relationship sparked me to do something that still has a positive effect on me today: I'm not hung up on social media, I changed my language, and by learning not to overthink, I became more patient with myself. Although something negative took place to get me here (and not saying it always has to be something bad), the fact is I got here! And I'm so much of a better, understanding, patient woman because of it. Secondly, I learned that real maturity is not waiting until some bad blow-up happens where tears and nasty words are being said.

On the contrary, God-sis it's having a mature conversation saying, "Hey, I love you, but right now, this isn't working for me, and to keep becoming who God is calling me to be, I need to let this go." It wasn't wise on my end to feel so unsettled and not say anything or overlook it because I was afraid of being alone. The best thing I could have done for that person was to be completely honest with them and myself. And honestly, it just wasn't working. No matter how much I want it to work and what I want the future to look like, if it isn't that, that's just what it is. My power lies in my present, not my past or the future. In many situations, we get caught up in the potential of a person that we miss *who they are.* It's more than okay to have a vision for someone or even see something in someone that usually helps. However, don't let it cloud your present and who they are showing you. Finally, I learned the difference between connecting and codependency. Although at the moment I felt I was connecting to another man, I realized I was in another co-dependent situation. As I mentioned earlier, I was anxious to jump into a new relationship instead of allowing God to bring me to the man. I was still stuck on taking pictures and capturing moments that I was still willing to accept, taking them with anyone. Although I thought I had moved from this, in this relationship, I learned I hadn't. Oh, and another thing, have you ever heard the phrase "love from a distance?" Well, this is a situation where I should've used that short, yet meaningful phrase.

As I mentioned earlier, he had an issue with anger. His temper would get the worst of him. And that just didn't work for me. By no means am I saying that you abandon people because they have issues. However, it is okay to mentally step back from someone if what they are doing is hurting you. That's not being selfish; that's taking care of you. God instructs you to take care of you. He says your body is a temple and to keep it holy. Well, your mind, body, and spirit operate as one, and if something is affecting you mentally, it will affect you physically. This man, his inconsistency, his emotional up and downs, his aura, his vibe, his spirit was causing me to change how I felt about myself but not in a good way. The moment it happened, it would have been wise for me to let him know that I'm willing to support him and connect him with the resources he needed, but dating romantically wasn't going to work for me. But I stayed, and everything I overlooked, in the beginning, became the reason it came to an end (thankfully).

Bottom line God-sis, trust yourself. God dwells within you. He is in You; you are connected and bound by His unconditional love. Listen to Him. He tells you when something is off. You can feel it at your center, your core, in your quiet place. At times we let what we want to overpower what God wants, but if we're honest: we essentially want the same thing. You want to be happy; God wants you to be happy, and you want love. God wants to give you that love you desire. Sometimes it's just a matter of God fine-tuning you. He prepares you for the thing you want. For instance, one week, I kept waking up at 5 am. I would just wake up and couldn't go back to sleep, no matter how early or late I went to sleep the night before. Finally, I thought: Is God trying to speak to me? Is there something He can't tell me during the day because I'm too busy or what? And I recognized during this hour of 5 am He had my full, undivided attention. So one morning, I woke up prepared this time with my journal and pen and just started writing what I felt God saying to me. He told me He wanted to give me everything I desired, but He needed me to be ready for it. You can want something and not be ready for it. And that's okay. It takes time. But these stepping stones are to prepare you to make you ready so that when you get what you're looking for, you can be ready. Let Him fine-tune you. Don't be anxious; simply be patient and trust that when it's your time, He'll give you the desires of your heart.

Reflection: Do you see things as only good or bad? Reflect on a situation that you once believed was negative. What did it teach you? How does it help you today?

STEP 6

Break the Cycles

If you are anything like me, God-sis, then you know what it's like to feel like the same thing just keeps happening in your life: the same situations, the same behavioral patterns, same mindsets, the same feeling of being stuck just comes out of nowhere. You think about it, pray about it, and then shortly after you're going through the same thing you just got out of. I started blaming other people in my life for the cycles I kept falling in.

I would think, "Well, my mom never taught me this, so this is just how I am."

Or "My dad did this, so this is why I'm this way."

I would even say, "I never saw this, so I don't know what it is."

If you're anything like me, God-sis, then let me tell you what I had to tell myself; it starts with you. I had to first come to a point where I stopped blaming people for the situations I allowed myself to be in.

"Oh, I've never seen my mother be single, so I don't know how to be single."

Girl, so what! So everything is your mother's fault now, and every bad relationship you've encountered is because of her? God-sis I have said before that everything is about balance and perspective. Yes, I agree that what you saw in your childhood shaped how you viewed life, marriage, friendships, and relationships. Yes, you do learn how to act from your parents or a parental figure in your life. Yes, they nurture your personality and how you think stems from what you see and what you experience. At the same time, there comes the point in time where you have to CHOOSE

FOR YOURSELF who you want to become and what you're going to take into the next dimensions of your life. Who you become from that point on is solely up to you. I used to blame people for everything that I believed was flawed about me. It's easy to blame and harder to take accountability. It's a coping mechanism to protect yourself. But I had to learn to swallow my pride and open up to God and let Him know that I found myself in toxic relationships because I didn't love myself. I had to get to the root of the issue, not the surrounding weeds.

The only way to break cycles or (psych-cules because it's in the mind) is to break it mentally, and one of the ways I learned to overcome it is with my speech. I changed what I said to myself, and I changed how I spoke to myself. I studied Sarah Jakes Roberts's messages and started reciting her powerful words. I started believing that I am not who my hurt says I am, but I'm who God says I am. I started believing that I am not who left me and that God still had a plan for my life. I also started seeking better counsel for myself. I started having conversations with people that weren't going to let me wallow in my dysfunction but make me boss up by giving me constructive criticism. I confided in trusted adults who guided me through my emotional frustrations. I just got tired of going in the same cycle. That's how the enemy gets you by keeping you in emotional, mental, and spiritual cycles. But instead of always telling God about my cycles, I told my cycles about God. He says I'm more than a conqueror. I also knew that once I broke it off of me, no other woman in my family nor my future daughters would have to break this off of them. Some of the cycles I dealt with personally were fear, doubt, overlooking when someone isn't treating me well out of the fear of being alone, this idea of not being whole and complete without a man, not feeling good enough, feeling worthless, using sex as a crutch, believing abuse was acceptable, operating in fear, pushing people away and also my skewed belief that I was too damaged to be loved.

Once again, God-sis, this is not something that I just moved past overnight; I still move past it till this day. Healing truly is an ongoing process and a journey that is not necessarily always a straight line. However, I make sure I move forward. For me, it didn't matter when the disconnect happened; I just know it happened, and it was going to end here. But not just for me. Sometimes what you go through has nothing to do with you. It can be for the people around you so they can see God's perfect hand on your life. You break that cycle not just for you but for your mother, for your sisters, for your children, for your future children, for your father, for your grandfather, for your cousins, for your friends! God needs representation, so be the example, be the standard! So what if the other people in your life missed the mark and didn't do it. YOU DO IT FOR YOU. HEAL FOR YOU. FORGIVE FOR YOU. Break the pattern! Are you aware that the word 'break' means an interruption of continuity or uniformity? And when I think of the word interruption, I automatically imagine two people talking, and then one person cuts the other person off mid-sentence resulting in the other person not being able to continue their thought. Do the same thing with your cycles. Interrupt them, don't let them continue to voice their opinions on to you or project anything on to you that does not align with what God says about you.

My favorite thing I always say is, "If it is not prospering you, LET IT GO!" If this way of thinking isn't working for you, change it. If this way of living isn't working for you, shift your atmosphere. Because where God is taking you, you can't afford to fall back into the same cycles. Breakthrough! Listen, God-sis I serve a God who will reward you for trying, He isn't impressed by your degrees or how many certifications you have; He's impressed by your heart, by your willingness to obey Him. He says your obedience will grow your heart. He knows that apart from Him, I can't do it. He knows I can get frustrated quickly. He knows when I operate from a place of fear that I produce anxiety, I become unsure and easily flustered. Yet, He still chooses me. He doesn't give up on me, so I REFUSE to give up on myself.

On the other hand, God-sis cycles can be very informative. If you pay attention, you can begin identifying what triggers you and what takes you back into that cycle. For me, it was fear. When I'm operating from a place of fear, everything I mentioned, like not feeling good enough, being unsure of myself, using sex as a crutch, overthinking, and negative thought patterns, will resurface.

So I would ask myself, "What is it you're afraid of?"

"What is causing you to revert backward?"

"What just took place to allow this to happen."

Once I identify the cause and the root, then seek wise counsel on how to overcome it. Sometimes I read, I watch a sermon, I sit in nature, or talk to a trusted adult or friend. Identifying it can be the hardest part because it involves admitting there's a disconnect, or something isn't working. At the same time, it's necessary and so much more beneficial because once you know what you're dealing with, you get the right tools to fight it.

Cycles can be hard, but like anything else, it's not impossible. Every once in a while, I have to get down and dirty with my cycles. I'll turn on Big Sean's famous breakup song, I Don't F*** With You, and sing it to every cycle trying to resurface itself. I remind myself that I've officially broken up with this way of thinking, this way of being, this way of operating. I reassure myself that I have overcome this, and those toxic traits had access to the old me. But ME, the new and improved Carla Ranee 2.0, doesn't have the time nor the energy to focus on something that's not going to prosper me.

Talkback to your cycles, God-sis! If they want to speak, interrupt them real quick, and remind them of who you are. Make the mental decision today that whatever is not prospering you, not benefiting you, not bringing you peace has to go, and just like an ex, you'll chuck the deuces and keep it moving.

Reflection: What cycles do you find yourself always in? Is it prospering for you? What are some ways you can break up with your cycles for good?

STEP 7

A Divine Connection

God-sis, throughout this book, you've seen me say that "when I operate in Him, I'm healed" or "in Him, I'm healed." The last step I would like to express to you is the most important. This step is how you can achieve all the others, but I wanted to save the best for last.

You are connected to God, and He is connected to you. However, are you using the power He has given you? It's like this: imagine in your mind someone jumping a car. One engine is alive, the other engine is asleep (let's not say dead). The two chords connect from the one engine that's alive to the other engine that is asleep; as one person goes to the engine that is working and starts the car, power, and energy, the electricity surges through the chords to the engine that is asleep.

However, the other person (in the car with the sleepy engine) has not turned their key, so the power from the other engine can wake up the other engine. All it takes to wake the sleeping engine is for the person to turn their key, and immediately, the connection is made, and life will burst within the engine. God-sis, I want you to think of this connection to the connection God wants to make with your heart. All He has attached to him like healing, forgiveness, sustainability, blessings, hope, power, love, freedom, understanding, and peace are all in His heart, and He longs to connect to yours.

After so many failed relationships, friendships, disappointments both left and right, it began to chip away at me and my engine, my spirit began to fall asleep. But when I finally said yes, and it wasn't a loud, dramatic yes but a quiet yes in my quiet place, to allow God to enter in my life, that was me turning the key and activating His power within me. His power, His peace, His love, His divine energy surged into my spirit, and a connection was made. I wasn't running on my own strength, but I began to wield His. When I made that connection, I was able to heal; forgive; GET UP 10, and Trust My Lonely. Uncertainty, I became aware that I needed to change my diet, I stopped letting sex control me. I learned to listen and broke cycles within myself that I longed to be free.

The Bible says in Psalms 34:8, "O taste and see that the LORD is good." AND I TASTED. SIS, I TASTED AND TORE IT UP! And now that I've tasted and learned for myself who God is, who I belong to, and the power I have, WHEW CHILE. There's nothing on this earth that can defeat me because my power doesn't come from anything in this world but comes from God within. I can also feel in my spirit when I disconnect from Him. You see, He will never disconnect from you. But there are times that we disconnect from Him. When I disconnect from Him and try to do things in my own strength, that's when I feel anxiety, that's when I feel afraid. Old habits begin to resurface because fear has taken place where Christ should be. Those are my symptoms. Your symptoms may be different.

When you surrender to God and His power, He teaches you who you are and shows you how you act when you try to stray from Him. God is within you, God-sis. The Kingdom dwells within, and all you have to do is stay connected. Turn your key. Seek Him first in all you do, and He will take care of you. He's not going to let you down. He can do everything BUT fail. It's not in His nature. And guess what? If God and I are connected, that means what applies to Him applies to me! Fear can't overtake Him; that means fear can't overtake me. He is love; I am love. He is more than a conqueror; I AM more than a conqueror. He is Joy; I am Joy in motion. (Now other things like being omnipotent and omnipresent that's all HIM, there's a reason why He's God. There are only things that He can do. I don't know about you, God-sis, but I can't be everywhere at once. I'd be TIRED with the little running around I do now). But when you activate that part of you that's connected to Him, you have access to that kind of power that tells cancer to back off, that commands the devil to back off of your finances, your peace of mind, your self-esteem, your purpose, your marriage, your relationship, etc. It also has allowed me to rest assured that no matter what happens next, God has already been there, so I know I'll be more than okay because ALL THINGS, not some things, not most things, but ALL THINGS work together for my good for those that love the Lord and are called according to His purpose.

GIRL, turn your key. Let His power wake you up. Recognize who you are. You don't have to do this walk on your own, and you *can't* do it on your own. You need God. Activate Him! He's waiting to give you the best of life, but you have to let Him. God is a gentleman, and He's not going to force Himself upon you; that's why He gave us the power of choice. Choose the One Man who will never leave you, never let you down, never give up on you, never criticize you, and will never make you feel bad about making a mistake or missing the mark. Turn your key and get ready to enjoy the ride of your life.

Reflection: Are you ready to turn your key? Why or Why not?

God-sis, it has been one beautiful journey. Thank you so much for taking the time to read my book. Thank you for not judging my life and allowing me to share it with you. I hope, in time, that this helps you. In some way, I pray you that become stronger than you were when you first opened this book. I hope it encourages you to keep pressing for everything you want in life. You can have it all; it just starts with you. Keep growing, keep laughing, keep loving, keep trying, keep failing, keep learning, and, most importantly, keep your eyes and mind on God. And whenever you need a reminder of God's glory, of His greatest creation, simply look in the mirror.

Until next time God-sis

Love, Carla Ranee

EPILOGUE

As I was returning home from Atlanta, I thought I was crying tears of disappointment, but God knew they were tears of joy. I thought I had lost my way, but God knew I had finally found my way. I thought it was the end, but God saw it was a new beginning. I thought I was starting over from scratch, but God saw I finally had a firm, solid foundation in which He could build upon. I thought I had done something wrong, maybe I didn't try hard enough to stay in Atlanta, but God knew my time was up, I learned what I needed to learn, and He had time to focus on my heart. I felt my heart was breaking, but God saw my heart was finally opening up and right where it needed to be.

As my dreams ended in Atlanta and I returned home, I thought I had lost everything. However, in returning home, I found everything. I got what I wanted, needed, prayed for, cried for, took losses for, grew for, overcame fear for, pushed, and endured for. And when I met him, I knew I tripped (literally) right into where God wanted me to be. I didn't understand at first, but God ended one path to place me on one where I could see the reflection of His love in another physical form. And God-sis he is everything I prayed for and more:

God brought me to my husband.

To be continued...

ABOUT THE AUTHOR/CARLA TILGHMAN

"Trust the process...your life can be falling apart and falling into place at the same time."

Born and raised in Delaware, Carla is the second born of five children. As a child, Carla was known for her bright demeanor and excelled at many things. At the age of 15-years-old, due to bullying, her mother enrolled her in the MISS MORALITY pageant, which focused on spiritual growth and the true meaning of being a woman of God. After going through three months of courses, workshops, and community service, Carla was crowned Queen in 2010, which blew her confidence out the water. From then, she applied to one of the best acting schools in the country in New York and received an $80,000 opportunity grant for school.

After earning her bachelor's degree in Acting, Carla embarked on her next journey to Florida to work for Walt Disney World Parks and Resorts. Soon after her internship ended, Carla chose to reflect and do some soul searching due to the painful situations that were occurring in her life at the time. Carla then switched gears to help other people focus on their mental health and be a light for women who are faced with challenges such as low self-esteem, hopelessness, and identity crisis. She then packed her bags and moved to Atlanta, Georgia, to pursue a master's in Clinical Mental Health Counseling to become a licensed professional. Carla is a certified Life Coach, guitar player, and loves all things self-care.

She lives by the quote, "Trust the process...your life can be falling apart and falling together at the same time," and in her life, God has shown her that this is all too true.

www.ingramcontent.com/pod-product-compliance
Lightning Source LLC
Chambersburg PA
CBHW062204100526
44589CB00014B/1950